Real Women Send Flowers

A CELEBRATION OF LIFE, LOVE, AND LUST

Susan Connaughton Curtin
and Patricia O'Connell
Illustrated by John Burgoyne

QUILL • NEW YORK • 1983

Library of Congress Catalog Card Number: 82-62321

ISBN: 0-688-02036-4(pbk)

Printed in the United States of America

First Quill Edition

1 2 3 4 5 6 7 8 9 10

Book Design by Liney Li

Special thanks to
Maggie Trichon and Marlene Sartini

Dedicated to Molly and Timothy Curtin
(two Real Children)

CONTENTS

Introduction

Real Women Send Flowers is a celebration of life, love, and lust. Today's real woman is gutsy. She has enough confidence to wear running shoes with a gabardine designer suit when she walks to work. The real woman does not wear white gloves and was not born with her legs crossed.

The real woman reads *Cosmo* for amusement, not guidance. She voted for the ERA and is not afraid of coed barracks. She jaywalks and whistles back at construction workers. Real women do not have names like Mimi, Pumpkin, Muffy, Buffy, Bunny, Tigi, Pandra, Patti Poo, Kitten, Binky, or Pinky. They do not answer to Babe, Baby, Hon, Sis, Toots, Sweetie, or Mam.

A real woman is secure enough in her own identity to take the name of the man she marries even though she may keep the name longer than the man.

A real woman loves men, but does not experience penis envy. She does not need a man to make herself credible and never refers to him as "my better half." She does not need to consult hubby or daddy before making a decision. Real women know how to cook and are proud of it. A real woman knows how to make and manage her own money, not just spend somebody else's. She is too busy to gossip but is often the subject of gossip. She sometimes eats junk food, goes on fad diets, and has cellulite.

Real women don't kiss and tell, especially for profit. When they walk into restaurants, they don't dance with the maître d' or perch themselves on the piano. Instead, they send food back if it is not prepared properly, and they know how to tip.

A real woman commands respect, she does not demand it. And finally . . . REAL WOMEN SEND FLOWERS.

"*That's right, I want the card to read
'Real women send flowers.'*"

"I used to be Snow White,

but I drifted."

—Mae West

Who Is
the
Real Woman?

❧✿❀

REAL WOMEN

Bette Davis

Barbara Walters

Jane Fonda

Miss Piggy

Katharine Hepburn

Tennessee Williams

Scarlett O'Hara

Barbara Bush

Anne Boleyn

Margaret Thatcher

Phil Donahue

Deborah Harry
(Blondie)

Meryl Streep

Jackie Kennedy
Onassis

Marie Antoinette

Barbara Woodhouse
(Mrs. Dog)

Diana Ross

Richard Simmons

Dolly Parton
(or so she says)

Joanne Woodward

Ruth Gordon

Lillian Hellman

Sara Lee

Lucille Ball

Lois Lane

Gloria Steinem

Brenda Starr

Cleopatra

Rose Fitzgerald Kennedy
*(give her a break,
she still has to
mother Teddy)*

Millicent Fenwick

Pearl Bailey

Ella Grasso

Lauren Bacall

Queen Mother

Bette Midler

Sandra Day O'Connor

Helen of Troy

Ellen Goodman

Golda Meir

Miss Lillian

Sarah Bernhardt

Coretta Scott King

The Go Go's

Alan Alda

Gertrude Stein

Madame

Diana Vreeland

Betty Friedan

Melina Mercouri

Simone Signoret

Carol Burnett

Jeanne Moreau

Pierre Trudeau

Simone de Beauvoir

Mae West

Julia Child

Snow White
*(she was no fool—she
had seven dwarves
waiting on her)*

WOMEN WHO ARE NOT REAL

Rosie Ruiz
*(nobody knows when
a real woman fakes it)*

Nancy Reagan

Truman Capote

Marie Osmond

Cinderella

Olivia Newton-John

Ralph Lauren

Winnie Winkle

Anita Bryant

Phyllis Schlafly

Barbara Mandrell

Tommy Tune

Ophelia

Margaret Trudeau

Kate Jackson
*(for her third marriage,
she and her husband
wore matching
jogging suits)*

Olive Oyl *(she whines)*

Cheryl Tiegs
*(real women don't want
their names on the
rear of anyone's jeans,
especially not Sears')*

Penelope

Cornelia Wallace

Mary Cunningham
*(real women don't feel
the need to get
annulments)*

Tammy Wynette

Jon Peters

June Cleaver
(Beaver's mother)

Annette Funicello
*(anyone over thirty
shouldn't be so pre-
occupied with peanut
butter)*

PEOPLE WHO THINK THEY ARE REAL WOMEN BUT ARE NOT

Renee Richards	Donny Osmond
Jim Bailey	Paul Williams
Bianca Jagger	Peter, Paul and Mary
Neil Sedaka	Mr. Rogers
Mia Farrow	Angie Dickinson
David Bowie	Burt Bacharach

NOT WORTH MENTIONING

Dr. Joyce Brothers

Bo Derek

Pia Zadora

Diane Keaton
(her only lasting relationship has been with her therapist)

Billie Jean King

Farrah Who?

Points to Ponder: Today's real woman is concerned and active. She philosophizes about burning
world issues and questions of grave importance,
such as:

POINT
TO
PONDER

#1

Is
spermicidal jelly
effective underwater
(especially in a hot tub)?

The Real Woman's Vocabulary

❦

R eal women say what they mean and mean what they say. They do not feel the need to converse in trendy, catchy, "valley girl" words or phrases. They do not use abbreviations like WASP, G & T, S & M, B & B, ACDC, or T & A. (The only acceptable abbreviations are M&M's and ET.)

Real women do not use real when they mean really.

When real women talk, people listen.

WORDS AND PHRASES NOT FOUND IN THE REAL WOMAN'S VOCABULARY

Painful, spiritual, camp, supportive, panache, karma, guilty, fantastic, wonderful, hopefully, awesome, funky, primal, intense, relevant, keen, unreal, interface, basically, adrenaline, charisma.

"You'll never guess what I did."

"Don't invade my space."

"Don't lay your power trip on me."

"I should have."

"Absolutely marvelous."

"What's your sign?"

"I could have died."

"Philosophically opposed to"

"I'm a feminist"
(*women who are don't need to announce it*).

"Trust me."

"How do you feel about us?"

"Consciousness raising"

"Let's discuss."

"I hear you."

"I know where you're coming from."

"It's better for both of us this way."

"What do you do?"

"I have to ask my husband first."

"My husband will kill me."

"I love it—I love it."

"I'll call you tomorrow"
(*better to send flowers*).

"Interesting" or "different" should never be used to describe a friend's avant-garde life-style, artwork, or lover.

WORDS AND PHRASES USED BY REAL WOMEN

Diaphanous, dazzling, clandestine, tumultuous, cryptic, asshole, pungent, androgyny, career planning, male-female relationships, assertiveness training, power, risk taking, professionalism, organizational barriers, strategies, conflict, enigma, cheeky, bold, and "Fuck 'em if they can't take a joke."

POINT
TO
PONDER

#2

Would a real woman
go out with
a man who thinks that
Aer Lingus
is a dirty word?

Appearance and Grooming

❧❦❧

Yesterday's ideal woman had platinum blond hair, big limpid eyes she batted frequently, and an IQ that matched her bust. Happily, those days, and that image, are gone, as women today are concerned with developing their brains, not just their busts. (A wise choice—overdeveloped breasts are a burden, but brains never sag, or cause backache.) The real woman is concerned but not obsessed with her appearance. She does not spend her evenings memorizing *Vogue*'s "250 ways to look great." She stays healthy, fit, and vital, and does not get hysterical at the sign of every wrinkle—and she does not go to anti-aging clinics.

Gone are the days of mixing eye of newt and toe of frog into a concoction that is supposed to beautify. And thanks to an arsenal of compact electrical appliances and hand-operated artillery, the makeover can be created with less effort and greater results.

A FEW WORDS ABOUT THE WELL-GROOMED WOMAN

Real women shave their legs and underarms.

Real women never have dirty toenails.

Real women use Right Guard deodorant and are not concerned with the masculine overtones of Irish Spring soap.

Real women do not tease, spray, or perform other unnatural acts upon their hair.

Real women never wear curlers in public.

Real women do not go to Merle Norman. Makeup is one thing, war paint is another.

A real woman does not pretend that she does not wear makeup; she does not think anyone is ignorant enough to believe that her eyelids are naturally purple and her lips strawberry glacé red. Real women don't put on makeup in the presence of men and don't walk around the house with Jolen Creme Bleach on their upper lips and eyebrows (life should have some mystery to it).

A real woman who wears contact lenses admits that she wears them out of vanity, not because they improve her vision. She does not need the aid of glasses to make her look more intelligent. Real women are intelligent.

*"If you haven't got
anything nice to say about anyone,
come sit by me."*

—Alice Roosevelt Longworth

WARDROBE

While the stain of original sin for all humanity was indeed a tragic aftermath of the Eden incident, let us not forget or downplay the second worst consequence—that nakedness was no longer "in," and ever since, women have been trying to find comfortable, practical, attractive alternatives.

Whalebone corsets, hoop skirts, spike heels, minis, midis, and maxis have all been the rage at one time or another; the collar-up-or-down controversy prevails.

Real women set trends; however, they do not follow them.

Pleasure from head to toe

REAL WOMEN DO NOT WEAR

Monogrammed sweaters (*real women know their own initials*)

Clothing with animals on it, particularly animals in rainbow colors performing unnatural acts (*e.g., blue squirrels carrying umbrellas*)

Anything turquoise

Buffalo sandals or huaraches

London Fog raincoats in pastel colors

Polyester pants suits

Spandex pants

Mini-skirts

Padded bras

T-shirts advertising the size of her breasts, the size of his penis, or anything else about body parts

Pom-pom socks

Lilly Pulitzer skirts

Pappagallo flats with zucchini blossoms on the toes

Anything from the Montgomery Ward catalog

Bermuda bags

Any career apparel creating the image of a Brooks Brothers clone in a skirt

Louis Vuitton handbags or luggage (*she does use old Vuitton trunks as coffee tables*)

Leslie Fay virgin dresses

Villager shirts with circle pins

White Stag ski parkas with coordinating pants

Anne Klein scarves and gloves

Gloria Vanderbilt stretch jeans

Jordache anything

Calvin Klein jeans

Lacoste

Ralph Lauren shirts (*who can afford his other clothes anyway?*)

Fendi bags (*the furs are o.k.*)

Anything by: Gucci, Pucci, or Fiorucci

Beene jeans

Pierre Cardin jeweled-neck sweaters

YSL jeans (*the perfume is great*)

REAL WOMEN DO WEAR

Softened career apparel

Natural fabrics, almost exclusively wool, silk, cotton, linen, cashmere, suede, and leather (*the latter not in the bedroom*)

An assortment of "Weekend at the Waldorf" lingerie

Silk underwear under jeans and a sweatshirt

Anything with pockets

Lanz nightgowns when they are cold and alone

Hanes (*because they fit well, not because gentlemen prefer them*)

L. L. Bean outerwear

Men's shirts and sweaters

Sweatpants in public

Old army raincoats

Khakis

Jeans (*their own*)

Well-bred old clothes

POINT
TO
PONDER

#3

Is it feminist
or feminine
to go braless?

The Bag Lady

A woman's handbag is the ultimate accessory and an absolute necessity. She does not leave home without it.

A real woman's bag is a modified version of one well prepared for a session of *Let's Make a Deal*. A real woman is ready for anything and her handbag is her survival kit.

"Why don't I give you my card."

THINGS YOU WOULD FIND IN A REAL WOMAN'S HANDBAG

A gold American Express card

Datebook (*not Hallmark*)

A diaphragm (*real women are not on the pill*)

Enough cash for a cab ride home from almost any-where

Passport (*real women are impulsive*)

A Swiss Army knife complete with tweezers, scissors, nail file, and corkscrew

Disposable razor

A twenty-four-hour money card

Address book containing the number of the local FTD florist

Mother-of-pearl fountain pen circa 1943 with no ink

Bidette premoistened towelette

THINGS YOU WOULD NOT FIND IN A REAL WOMAN'S HANDBAG

Handkerchief

Binaca

Hairy brush

Tissues with lipstick blots

Matching wallet and makeup case

Theme notepad with attached pencil

Vivarin

Picture of hubby and the kids

Sorority group photo

A change of underwear (*real women would go without*)

Tampon containers in harvest-gold or avocado

Education

T oday's real woman knows that the acquisition of a BA is not one of life's absolute essentials. Eleanor Roosevelt never attended college, nor did Virginia Woolf; Golda Meir and Sandra Day O'Connor did. Real women go to school at any age.

SCHOOLS REAL WOMEN DO ATTEND

Night schools

MIT

Harvard

University of California at Berkeley

Oberlin

NYU

Yale

Princeton

Summer schools in foreign countries

Real women do not attend colleges like Wheaton or Wheelock or other schools that sound like breakfast cereals.

EDUCATIONAL INSTITUTIONS NOT WORTH ATTENDING

Barbizon or any facsimile thereof

Bartending school

FIT

All junior colleges
(*that means two-year schools*)

ICS schools of bookkeeping, art, and fashion merchandising (*picture the campus in Scranton*)*

North American School of Animal Sciences
(*learn to be a zookeeper at home in your spare time*)

Lural
(*be a lady in white*)

Regina Careers Limited
(*become a stained-glass artist on the "Round Lake Campus"*)

*No salesman will call!

Real Careers
for Women

❧⟡❧

O kay, so Jane Fonda is a tough act to follow. Not everyone can be intelligent and aware, beautiful and perfectly toned, run a successful business, write best sellers, win Academy Awards, and be a supportive wife and mother. So, OK, Jane is terrific, and doing great, and so are the rest of the real women. They are:

Scuba divers, not pearl divers—there must be an easier way to get that necklace.

Teachers because they want to be, not because they can't do anything else.

Models because they can make large amounts of money and have a lot of spare time, not for ego reinforcement.

Sports reporters, not Dallas cowgirls.

Housewives and mothers because they choose to be.

Secretaries

Waitresses

Hookers

Physicians

Truck drivers

Masseuses

Shepherds (never sheep)

Animal trainers in the circus

Racing-car drivers or mechanics
(*real women don't care if they meet Paul Newman*)

Dentists
(*even though everyone hates them*)

Lawyers

Lumberjacks
(*not lumberjills*)

Airline pilots

Historical-fiction writers
(*not Harlequin Romance writers*)

Real women do not run cute shops as tax deductions for their husbands.

Real women do not own health-food stores with names like The Tofu Experience.

Shepherds (*never sheep*)

"Mistress!

What would I get out

of that except

a passel of brats?"

—Scarlett O'Hara's
reply to Rhett Butler

POINT
TO
PONDER

#4

Is
Princess Di
a
real woman?

The Real Woman's Guide to Love and Lust

🍀🌿🍀

A real woman is not afraid to DO IT on the first date. She doesn't care if he respects her in the morning.

Real women are good in bed.

Real women send flowers the next day.

Real women never apologize about their breast size (they know that anything more than a handful is superfluous).

Real women don't read HOW TO books on sex.

When real women choose to have affairs with married men, they come away enriched, not embittered.

Real women have never been and never will be THE TOWN PUMP (real women are selective).

Real women know how to masturbate. It's unemotional, needs no birth control, and there is no one to make breakfast for the next morning.

Real women will try anything, at least once, with another consenting adult.

Real women don't believe that any body is better than no body.

Real women are always supportive and understanding when their lovers say, "This has never happened to me before."

A real woman does not buy a vibrator and pretend it is for her face, scalp, or ankle.

A real woman lives with a man if she chooses to even if her mother tells her, "He won't buy the cow if he can get the milk for nothing."

Real women do not invite men over for Harvey's Bristol Cream.

A real woman does not care if she is seen with a married man—it's his problem, not hers.

Real women do not screw in bathrooms on airplanes, particularly with men they have just met.

Real women do not need Vaseline for any reason.

A real woman will not sleep with a man just because he has spent money on her.

A real woman will sleep with a man who has not spent a dime on her, if she is so inclined.

Real women assume their parents still have sex.

Real women don't need to be on top.

A real woman takes a cab home (any distance) rather than spend the night with someone when she doesn't want to.

Real women talk dirty in bed.

Real women are dirty in bed. According to Woody Allen, "If it's not dirty, you're not doing it right."

REAL WOMEN DO NOT PARTAKE IN MULTI-PLE-MARRIAGE CEREMONIES PERFORMED BY REVEREND AND MRS. MOON, EVEN THOUGH IT MAY BE A "PROFOUNDLY PERSONAL AND RELIGIOUS EXPERIENCE."

LINES REAL WOMEN NEVER FALL FOR

"My wife doesn't understand me."

"I like you a lot; it's just that I'm skittish about relationships."

"I won't come in your mouth."

"I'll sleep on the wet spot."

"I won't put it in—I'll just rub it up and down."

"We don't have to do anything."

"We can just lie here with our clothes off."

LINES REAL WOMEN DON'T GIVE MEN (UNLESS THEY'RE TRUE)

"I've never seen one that big."

"Of course it was wonderful for me too."

"No one has ever done that to me before."

"I usually don't gag."

"I'll send flowers."

"If you need anything

just whistle.

You know how to whistle,

don't you, Steve?

Just put your lips together

and blow."

—Lauren Bacall

in *To Have and Have Not*

THINGS REAL WOMEN DON'T WEAR IN THE BEDROOM

Curlers

Mudpacks

Cold cream

Moustache bleach

Cotton nightgowns

Anything their mothers gave them (especially pink flannel)

Quilted bathrobes

Cotton spanky pants

Socks

THEY DO WEAR

Well-cut silk pajamas

Any invisible night cream

Garter belts with silk stockings

Men's robes in silk or wool

Cologne

Teddies

A provocative smile

TEN THINGS TODAY'S WOMEN LOOK FOR IN A MAN

1. Vasectomy scars

2. Intelligence

3. Time

4. A sense of humor

5. A deceased mother

6. A vase

7. A steady job with room for advancement

8. Good teeth

9. A hard body

10. Good demographics

REAL WOMEN
NEVER GO OUT
WITH MEN

Whose hair is longer than theirs, or who spend more to get it cut than they do.

Whose jeans have more decorations on their pockets than their own.

Who spend more time to get ready than they do (particularly if there is limited bathroom space).

Whose heels are higher than theirs, or whose cologne is stronger, or who wear more jewelry than they do.

And finally, real women never, ever, go to bed with men who weigh less than they do—it is just too intimidating!

EIGHT THINGS
A REAL WOMAN WOULDN'T
DO ON A DATE

1. Wait for a man to open the car door.

2. Insist on ordering for herself (*a real woman has too many important decisions to make in her life to worry about the trivial ones*).

3. Order the least expensive thing on the menu.

4. Talk about former lovers.

5. Talk about Daddy.

6. Hint that she would love for him to send her flowers.

7. Hum songs like "When Will I Be Loved?" or "Call Me" (a real woman would call him).

8. Tell him that her biological time clock is running out.

*"I think I should tell you, Freddy,
I've had breast reduction surgery."*

FIVE THINGS A REAL WOMAN WOULD DO THE NEXT MORNING

FIVE THINGS A REAL WOMAN WOULD NOT DO THE NEXT MORNING

1. An encore.

1. Ask "When will I see you again?"

2. Lend him her toothbrush.

2. Hang around waiting for flowers to come.

3. Tell him how she likes her eggs.

3. Get an answering service so she won't miss his calls.

4. Assure him that she still respects him.

4. Order a subscription to *Bride's Magazine.*

5. Send flowers.

5. Add his mother to her Christmas list.

POINT TO PONDER

#5

Do
real women
send flowers
the second time?

The Real Woman and Parties

Real women are social creatures. They love to give parties. They arrive late and stay late. Real women are highly selective about the parties they attend. A real woman never goes to Mary Kay cosmetic parties, Tupperware parties, or tailgate parties. She attends fund-raisers, lingerie parties (where she can buy that "Weekend at the Waldorf" lingerie) and cocktail parties. A real woman does not mind being the extra woman at a party or going without a date. She realizes that she is attending a social function, not a reenactment of Noah's Ark. If the real woman is not visible at a party, it is for one of the following reasons:

1. She is in the kitchen, which is where the most interesting people converge. Also, being in the kitchen gives one first and last crack at the food.
2. She is sitting off in a quiet corner, talking with the person she has determined to be the most interesting, regardless of age, sex, and the gossip that may ensue.
3. She left, because she was bored, tired, or met somebody to whom she might send flowers the next day.

WHAT REAL WOMEN DRINK AT PARTIES

Real women drink champagne anytime, not just on New Year's Eve.

Real women drink white wine (red wine stains teeth, linen, and clothing).

Real women drink imported beer out of the bottle.

Real women drink Twinings loose tea made in a heated pot (leave the tea bags for Chris Evert Lloyd and Don Meredith, and other Lipton-tea lovers).

Black coffee—real women didn't fall for Carol Lawrence's instant fakes.

REAL WOMEN DO NOT

Drink pink drinks with cherries.

Drink cocktails through straws.

Order drinks with onions in them—no matter how small and cute the onions are.

Make drinks with Holland House mixers or buy premixed cocktails for two. Convenience foods are one thing, convenience drinks are another.

Real women do not drink Perrier—it gives gas.

And finally, real women do not say yes to Martini & Rossi.

THINGS REAL WOMEN DO AT PARTIES

1. Bring food.
2. Tell dirty jokes in mixed company.
3. Flirt with married men.
4. Stay to help clean up.
5. Ask men for their phone numbers.

THINGS REAL WOMEN DO NOT DO AT PARTIES

1. Discuss feminine protection.
2. Play charades.
3. Pretend to understand jokes that they really don't.
4. Compare their children, their children's schools, and their children's pictures.

THE REAL WOMAN GIVES A PARTY

Real women do not consult Amy Vanderbilt's complete guide to etiquette when giving a party; they trust their instincts.

Real women do not have theme parties, and do not invite couples only, or people who will "just love each other." They do not use paper tablecloths and napkins, especially ones with themes and motifs on them. They do not have place cards done in calligraphy, and do not serve Irish coffee in glasses with shamrocks all over them that say "Irish coffee."

Real women do not serve food in tinfoil sculptures, made to resemble the animal of the food's origin.

Real women do not shake and bake, stir and frost, or brown and serve.

FOODS REAL WOMEN DO NOT SERVE AT PARTIES

Pigs-in-blankets, meatballs, especially Swedish ones, tripe, tongue, roast suckling pig (except for Greek Easter), any breaded frozen foods, deviled eggs, any casserole, flaming apple omelette, mustard mousse, magical mango, puree of peas, steak tartare—have you ever kissed a man after he has had this? It's like having your dog lick you after

he's eaten Ken-L-Ration—hamburger that has
been helped, California onion dip, potato chips,
pretzels, Triscuits, fondue, Jell-O, Ritz crackers
(contrary to popular belief, nothing tastes better
when it's sitting on a Ritz), tofu, Wonder bread,
any one of the twenty-one impossible pies made
with Bisquick.

FOODS REAL WOMEN DO SERVE AT PARTIES

Fresh fruits, vegetables, baba au rhum, trifle, sal-
ade niçoise, charlotte russe, anything the local
caterer can mass-produce on short notice, ripe,
oozing-off-the-plate Brie, Norwegian flat bread,
caviar (one food that can't be bought faked, frozen,
or canned), pâté, anything made with fresh
seafood.

Dijon French mustard (not French's mustard).
Fresh turkeys (not frozen butterballs with built-in
thermometers).
Salted nuts (what good are dried or roasted nuts?).
Chocolate-chip brownies.
Godiva chocolates.
Any Häagen-Dazs ice cream.

The Real Woman's Guide to Rest and Relaxation

❧❀❧

Real women play poker, not bridge. They do not join clubs like The Ace of Clubs or The Out-to-Lunch Bunch. Instead, they belong to the college club of their alma mater, women's networks, professional clubs, and the Sierra Club.

Real women are never found at a piano bar, attired in tasteful career apparel, draped over other young professionals, singing "What I Did for Love."

A real woman is not seen walking down the street "listening to Vivaldi" on her Sony Walkman, and "really getting off on it."

SPORTS AND HOBBIES

A few words about sports and leisure-time activities.

The real woman is not afraid of being too strong or having muscles. She plays squash, and baseball with her kids, and she does Nautilus (not Gloria Stevens). She jumps rope, paces while talking on the phone, and jogs—but not as much as she promises herself she will.

She skis, snorkels, swims, and windsurfs. (It tones those hard-to-reach areas.)

Real women care whether they win or lose, not what they look like when they play the game.

SPORTS NOT ENGAGED IN BY REAL WOMEN

Bowling (especially in leagues)   Golf

Racquetball (it's too trendy)   Paddle tennis

                                              Disco

MOVIES

People used to wait eagerly for the release of a movie; now they just wait for it to be shown on television. Even though being able to get real butter on your popcorn is a big advantage to watching a movie at home, there are still some movies real women consider worth seeing.

MOVIES REAL WOMEN WOULD GO SEE

Norma Rae	How Green Was My Valley
Julia	Cabaret
Gone With the Wind	The Wizard of Oz
The Turning Point	Zorba the Greek
Anything Rex Reed does not like	Anything with Lauren Bacall
Casablanca	The Philadelphia Story
Starting Over	All About Eve
To Have and Have Not	The Misfits
Jezebel	She Done Him Wrong
My Brilliant Career	On Golden Pond
ET	

REAL WOMEN WOULD NOT SEE

Anything starring Clint Eastwood

Movies with subtitles—real women are too sensible to read in the dark

Any movie with slow motion, or that ends in a freeze frame

Porno movies, except for once, out of curiosity

Movies with rodents, insects, disasters, vegetables, or inanimate objects as the central characters

Any Blondie, Gidget, or James Bond movies

"Gimme a viskey.

And a chincher ale on the side.

And don't be stingy, baby."

—Greta Garbo

in *Anna Christie*

TELEVISION

Television as a sophisticated means of communication cannot be ignored, although it has not always been the real woman's best friend. The fifties flooded the black and white screen with horrendous role models who were obviously the perverted fantasies of male writers. The audience was presented with a bevy of contented housewives, tastefully attired in shirtwaist dresses with the requisite string of ladylike pearls at the neck. These women selflessly gave their time, love, and endless supplies of freshly home-baked chocolate-chip cookies to their families, who took it all for granted. With beatific smiles, Harriet Nelson, Donna Reed, June Cleaver, Loretta Young, Jane Wyatt, and June Lockhart carried us through those formative years.

A real woman is too busy to spend a lot of time watching TV and no longer looks toward it for her role model. She does occasionally retire to the tube on those occasions when she is in need of amusement, enlightenment, or escape. However, a real woman would never tape soap operas on her Betamax. (There are lots of better uses for video equipment.)

A real woman does not watch football, baseball, basketball, golf, or Ping-Pong on television unless she is really interested. She does not sit in front of the television just to be "near her man."

Real women do not say "I don't even own a TV" or "I never watch TV."

SHOWS A REAL WOMAN WOULD WATCH

The *Today* show: It's not easy to come by cheerful, intelligent conversation before 9:00 A.M.

Phil Donahue

60 Minutes

Barbara Wa Wa specials

Wild World of Animals

Macy's Thanksgiving Day Parade

Reruns of *Saturday Night Live* with the old cast

20/20

Reruns of *I Love Lucy* (Lucy was the only real woman on television for years)

6 P.M. local news

7 P.M. national news

Laverne & Shirley

Reruns of *The Mary Tyler Moore Show*, before Rhoda left

Public television (real women are secure enough to admit when they are bored by it)

*M*A*S*H*

Hill Street Blues

REAL WOMEN DO NOT WATCH

The Brady Bunch

The John Davidson Show

Mister Rogers

Hawaii Five-O

Reruns of Charlie's Angels

Reruns of Kojak

The Fall Guy

Dallas (real women didn't care who shot J.R.)

Game shows

Alice (real women do not stop over in Phoenix for five years en route to Hollywood)

Soap operas (well, not all the time)

Real People

Solid Gold

Love Boat

Fantasy Island

Three's Company

One Day at a Time

The Merv Griffin Show

"Miss Universe" Pageant

Times Square on New Year's Eve

Low-budget made-for-TV movies

THE REAL WOMEN'S GUIDE TO SHOPPING

It cannot be overlooked that the real woman's greatest source of relaxation is SHOPPING, be it for clothing or antiques (never for groceries).

DO'S AND DON'TS

They don't go to Bloomie's on Saturday morning (it's Bloomie's, not Bloomingdale's).

They do shop by mail from:
    Bloomie's
    L. L. Bean
    Ann Taylor
    Tiffany's
    Neiman-Marcus
    Royal Silk and Horchow catalogs whenever
        possible.

Do go antique shopping but are not intimidated by auction dealers.

Do spend the day at Tiffany's (look what it did for Audrey Hepburn).

Don't look for bargains at Macy's.

Do shop at Loehmann's.

Do hit Rodeo Drive (when the budget allows).

Do lunch at the Bird Cage and Palm Court.

Do go to junk stores.

REAL WOMEN WILL ALWAYS BE SHOPPERS.

POINT
TO
PONDER

#6

Do real women engage in
telephone sex?
If so, would they have
Dial-a-Fantasy
on the list of
emergency phone numbers?
(In other words,
is long distance really
the next best thing
to being there?)

The
Well-Read Woman

A real woman escapes with *Town and Country*, not a Harlequin Romance. She reads for enjoyment and relaxation, and knows a good book is something that she can take to bed with her that does not expect breakfast in the morning, or flowers the next day.

In addition to the books in her library, which range from childhood favorites to classics, a real woman reads *The Sunday New York Times*, *The Wall Street Journal*, *Barron's*, any publication related to her career, and instruction books that come with appliances.

A real woman does not read her husband's mail or her children's diaries. She never even opens *Reader's Digest* and does not buy tabloid newspapers that have articles like "I died, and lived to tell about it." A real woman does not read Petticoat Pornography or books that use nouns like rake and verbs like ravish and have heroes with names like Basil, Alistair, or Titus.

Books Found in a
Real Woman's Library

FICTION:

Madame Bovary

Gone With the Wind
(historical, romantic, and a great source of ideas
for "what to do with old drapes")

Catcher in the Rye

Fanny Hill:
Memoirs of a Woman of Pleasure

Where the Sidewalk Ends

Marjorie Morningstar

Little Women

Valley of the Dolls

Middlemarch

Jane Eyre

War and Peace

The Brothers Karamazov

Candide

The Good Earth

Alice in Wonderland

The Group

Thin Thighs in Thirty Days
(how can the achievements of a lifetime be undone
in a mere month?)

A Room of One's Own

Fear of Flying

Anything by Sidney Sheldon

Ulysses
(real women do not pretend to have read or understood it all)

The Scarlet Letter
(contrary to popular belief, this is not a history of the monogrammed sweater)

NONFICTION:

The Kama Sutra

The Female Eunuch

Sylvia Porter's Money Book for the Eighties

The Cinderella Complex

Linda Goodman's Sun Signs

Our Bodies, Ourselves

Out of This Century

Whistling Girl

Women's Whole Earth Catalogue

Toward a New Psychology of Women

HUMOR:

How to Eat Like a Thin Person
The Total Woman

BOOKS NOT FOUND IN A REAL WOMAN'S LIBRARY

Any self-help books of the seventies
The Story of O
Anything by Rosemary Rogers or Barbara Cartland
Eileen Ford's Book of Model Beauty
Masters and Johnson
How to Flatten Your Stomach
Any Dale Carnegie book
Any Dieter's Guide to Weight Loss Before, During, or After Sex
The Dance-Away Lover
Open Marriage and its sequel
I'm OK, You're OK
How to Be Your Own Best Friend
How to Make Love to a Man
The Total Orgasm
Suburban Souls
The Best of Dear Abby
A Woman's Body: An Owner's Manual
Am I a Good Lover?
Secrets of the Super Beauties
Shared Intimacies
Total Sexual Fitness for Women
What Every Woman Should Know About a Man
The Cosmo *Report*

COOKBOOKS FOUND IN A REAL WOMAN'S KITCHEN

The Joy of Cooking

The Settlement Cookbook

The New York Times Cook Book

Greek Cooking for the Gods

Betty Crocker's Cookbook

Anything by Julia Child or James Beard

COOKBOOKS NOT FOUND IN A REAL WOMAN'S KITCHEN

101 Uses for Hamburger

The Whole Grain Cookbook

Any Junior League or Chamber of Commerce collection of favorite recipes

Weight Watchers International Cookbook

Any manufacturer-sponsored cookbook

The Teflon Guide to Not Getting Stuck in the Kitchen

More Recipes from the Backs of Boxes, Bottles, Cans, and Jars

The I Love New York Diet, or any other geographic diet book (real women do not go on regional diets)

Cookbooks featuring recipes from celebrities (who cares what Jimmy Carter does with his peanuts?)

"Come up and see me sometime.

Come up Wednesday.

That's amateur night."

—Mae West

The Real Woman Goes on Holiday

❧❦❧

T he real woman travels in style. She travels with a good deal of luggage, but never with more than she can handle. (Porters and willing gentlemen are usually in short supply.) The "Wardrobe on Wheels" is an absolute must, and is packed with the essentials: any and all electrical appliances, and an ample supply of nonwrinkling clothing that goes everywhere and does nearly everything. (Polyester is very tacky and should be avoided at any cost.) The real woman blends in with the locals, she does not scream "turista." She prefers to travel off season, to avoid the hordes of tourists.

A real woman will not be found at Grossinger's, Club Med, or in the Hamptons, and she goes to Nantucket or Martha's Vineyard only in the fall. She doesn't go anywhere that Gidget went and she does not cruise on Love Boat in search of Mr. Right. She will never be found in Las Vegas, Miami Beach, or Atlantic City.

PLACES REAL WOMEN GO ON HOLIDAY

Summer schools in foreign countries

Klosters, Switzerland

The Galápagos Islands

Majorca

Pepperidge Farm

New York (because it's big and exciting, not in spite of that fact)

The Aran Islands

Bali, Indonesia

The South of France (not in August)

Portugal

Greece and the Islands

Woodstock, Vermont (not Woodstock, New York, as a pilgrimage)

Ashtabula, Ohio

P-town

The Poconos (portable video equipment and heart shaped bathtubs are wasted on newlyweds) bring a partner.

Chappaquiddick (only once)

Scientific research expeditions anywhere (tax-deductible)

Kenya

Portillo, Chile, in the summer for winter skiing

Disney World

Real Women
Have Drive

Real women are savvy drivers. They pump
their own gas and know how to change their
own oil and flat tires, but they also know how to get
it done for them. A real woman does not adorn her
car with personal license plates and/or bumper
stickers advertising her personal preferences in
politics, pets, or philosophy.

A real woman's personality is imprinted on the
interior of her car, not the exterior.

THINGS THAT WOULD BE FOUND
IN A REAL WOMAN'S CAR

Crumpled coffee cups from Dunkin' Donuts

Chipwich wrappers

A squash racquet

Plaid wool blanket with fringe

Clothes that should have gone to the dry cleaner
three months ago

$5 for emergency money in the glove compartment

One glove under the seat that she has been seriously looking for for a considerable amount of time

A driver's manual, still in the original wrapper, which has never been looked at

Dog hairs

One yellow and one red plastic sand pail left over from the kid's holiday at the beach—can be used for ice buckets while traveling

THINGS YOU WOULD NOT FIND IN A REAL WOMAN'S CAR

Greek worry beads, or anybody's graduation tassel hanging over the mirror

St. Christopher or any other plastic statue suctioned onto the dashboard

Telephone (too pretentious)

A computerized horn that plays the opening lines to ninety-eight different songs

Fur steering-wheel cover

REAL WOMEN DRIVE

Ten-speed bicycles

Mercedeses

Land-Rovers

Porsches

Army surplus Jeeps

Jaguars

Honda Accords

Old cars with sentimental value

Their own planes

A REAL WOMAN IS NEVER FOUND BEHIND THE WHEEL OF THE FOLLOWING VEHICLES

Pink or any other color Cadillac

VW buses

Gas-guzzling Jeep Wagoneers (for the rides up-country)

Volvo station wagons

Oldsmobile station wagons with wood panels on the side (gift from hubby)

Golf carts

Bright Moments in the History of Real Women

Herodias requests the head of John the Baptist on a silver platter as a wedding gift, thus initiating The Bridal Registry.

Cleopatra sends Mark Antony a papyrus plant— earliest record of a woman sending a man flowers.

Delilah cuts Sampson's hair (real women don't go out with men whose hair is longer than theirs).

Helen of Troy's face launches a thousand ships.

Attila the Hun, the great warrior, dies in action in the boudoir, not on the battlefield. (Is the penis not mightier than the sword?)

Mary, Queen of Scots, gets rid of her boring husband, instituting the concept of throwaway husbands.

Marie Antoinette says, "Let them eat cake," introducing junk food as a viable alternative to wholesome, well-balanced meals.

The Statue of Liberty is erected, America's first ambassadress and subsequent role model for the Welcome Wagon lady.

The first mail-order catalog—women are now able to spend money without leaving home.

Greta Garbo says to John Barrymore, in the movie *Grand Hotel*, "I want to be alone."

The first Toll House cookie is baked.

Introduction of the tampon.

Invention of permanent press.

Jackie Kennedy suggests Acapulco as the perfect place for the Democratic Convention.

The Beatles write and record "I Wanna Be Your Man."

*Liberation from girdles as control-top panty hose offers women a more comfortable means to a flatter stomach.

Invention of electric curlers. (Women no longer had to sleep with orange-juice cans in their hair in order to create the perfect bouffant.)

The opening of the first twenty-four-hour supermarket.

Reddi-Wip comes on the market (first food in an aerosol can).

Introduction of instant coffee, first powdered caffeine in a jar.

The gas grill becomes a permanent fixture all over America. Men could take over barbecuing year round, regardless of prevailing weather conditions.

Fear of Flying is published. The first sexually frank novel written by a woman, admitting that women, too, have "lust in their hearts."

"Call waiting" becomes available, making the busy signal obsolete.

Telephone company introduces "Call forwarding." For a mere $2.70 a month real women can now forward their obscene phone calls to Dial-a-Prayer.

*Future Bright Moment in History—invention of inner-thigh-control pantyhose.

Bleak Moments in the History of Real Women

Eve gets blamed for Adam's eating the apple, thus forever dooming women to menstrual cramps and having to worry about what they wear.

The Crusades—first business trip where the wife is left home with the kids for an extended period of time.

Droughts in Europe cause a shortage of flowers. Women are forced to send candy instead.

Jack the Ripper terrorizes London, making it impossible for hard-working women to walk the streets.

The birth of Phyllis Schlafly.

The Duke of Windsor abdicates the British throne for Wallis Warfield Simpson (the woman he loved), and the two become the most boring professional dilettante couple in history.

The long-line bra is invented, a body harness that cuts off circulation to the brain.

The Twiggy look becomes popular, forcing women

to swear off M&M's for an extended period of time.

Sylvia Plath writes: "Every woman adores a fascist."

National Airlines launches its "Fly Me Girls" advertising campaign, perpetuating the "coffee, tea or me" image.

Looking for Mr. Goodbar is released, a film that gives casual sex a bad name.

Elizabeth Taylor divorces Richard Burton for the second time, disproving the theory that husbands can be recycled.

Billie Jean King admits having an affair with her secretary. First time a woman admits to doing so.

Nancy Reagan says: "If Ronnie were a shoe salesman, I'd be out there selling shoes too."

Mary Cunningham marries William Agee, despite the fact that they were just "good friends."

Real Women as Mothers

Real mothers:

Listen to their kids.
Play with their kids.
Yell at them.
Make homemade chicken soup for them.
Hug and kiss their kids.
Respect them and love them.

Real mothers never tell dirty or racial jokes in front of children.

Real mothers never embarrass their kids in front of their friends.

Real mothers are smart enough to let their kids do their own homework.

Real mothers wear what their children gave them for Christmas and birthdays.

Real mothers never throw out their kids' artwork.

Real mothers never give their daughters dolls with names like Growing-up Skipper that grow one inch in the torso and have breasts that pop out with the mere rotation of an arm.

Real mothers never spell things out in front of their kids or talk in pig Latin.

*"What time will you be home
from school today, Mom?"*

REAL MOTHERS NEVER TELL THEIR CHILDREN:

1. You were delivered by the stork, or You grew in the garden.

2. Your freckles are beautiful and will disappear when you turn thirteen.

3. That's just baby fat; it will go away.

4. The boogieman will get you.

5. Eating carrots will make your hair curly and allow you to see in the dark.

6. Eat everything on your plate or you won't get dessert.

7. I'll tell your father.

8. Hair will grow on your hands.

9. Because I said so; I'm your mother.

10. It hurts me more than it hurts you.

QUESTIONS REAL MOTHERS WILL HAVE TO ANSWER

1. Where did I come from? (Before you give a lengthy answer on human sexuality, find out if they mean region of the country.)

2. Are Bert and Ernie gay, and if not, why have they lived together for so many years and slept in the same bedroom?

3. Am I your slave? (This generally occurs when you request that clothing be picked up off the bedroom floor.)

4. What year did you get married? (Be sure you make this at least nine months prior to the first child's birthday.)

5. Numerous impossible history questions.

6. Do you love Daddy?

7. Why do you lock the bedroom door?

8. How do you spell antidisestablishmentarianism?

9. What does FUCK mean?

10. Did they have cars when you were little?

11. Did you have to wear braces?

"Gentlemen prefer blondes,

but who says

blondes prefer gentlemen?"

—Mae West

Real Women Send Flowers

❀᭜᭜❀

MEN TO WHOM REAL WOMEN WOULD SEND FLOWERS

Paul Newman	Mikhail Baryshnikov
Alan Alda	Ed Asner
Tom Brokaw	Luciano Pavarotti
Kris Kristofferson	Kermit the Frog
Ricardo Montalban	Tom Selleck
Bryant Gumbel	Johnny Carson
George Plimpton	Norman Lear
Willie Nelson	Al Pacino
Richard Burton	Harrison Ford
Starsky and Hutch	John Forsythe
Jon Voight	Jason Robards
Woody Allen	Peter Falk
Mick Jagger	Superman

MEN TO WHOM REAL WOMEN WOULD NOT SEND FLOWERS

Richard Harris

The Dukes of Hazzard

Tom Jones
(*he'd be expecting them*)

Marlon Brando and George C. Scott
(*they might refuse to accept them*)

Robert Redford
(*he might accuse you of upsetting the ecological balance*)

John Denver
(*he's a little too sensitive*)

William Agee
(*he'd lie about receiving them*)

Richard Nixon
(*he'd say he knew nothing about it*)

FIVE MEN YOU COULD TORTURE BY SENDING FLOWERS AND NOT SIGNING THE CARD

1. **Warren Beatty**
2. **Joe Namath**
3. **Erik Estrada**
4. **Ryan O'Neal**
5. **Burt Reynolds**

POINT
TO
PONDER

#7

Do real women care if it was
good for him, too?

Some Thoughts About Real Men

Real men are secure enough to wear pink.

Real men are not afraid to have vasectomies.

Real men make great coffee and know how to do their own laundry.

Real men don't get permanents.

Real men are not intimidated by women who drive faster or more expensive cars than they do.

Real men don't let Musk cologne by English Leather speak for them; real men speak for themselves.

Real men don't get manicures.

Real men are interested in learning new things; they are not threatened by women who have more sexual experience than they.

Real men are touched when women send them flowers.